The Remaining Years

The Remaining Years

The Remaining Years

Poems by

Bridget Sprouls

Cover art by Bridget Sprouls

ISBN: 978-1-949229-78-3

Kelsay Books
Aldrich Press
www.kelsaybooks.com

For Waleed, who kept showing up

Contents

Hermit

There is an errand boy across the stream,
waiting with another day's loaf of distant sweetness.

We do nothing, such as grope the trees' buttery fruit,
tipple nectar from sprawling, chomp-orange blossoms.

A leaf blows down, and for a moment, one of us has perished.

The boy didn't know he could block light
until one day he wandered far from home,
stood very still, and watched.

Sometimes a mallet cloud hangs over him,
and his eyes swell into the most fragile porcelain.

This is when I part the curtains
and effort my skull transparent enough that he may see himself
limping his route through the usual valleys,
an untamed ripple,
a worthy blot frittering gloriously behind schedule,
the air behind him rolling with pollen—or is it grief?—
and around us the gnarled roots
become simply curious.

*

On the side of the stream where I misplaced everything,
the man of dead leaves
stands on his outcrop,

the gloom around him a constant last glance.

It used to scare me when a gust of wind loosed parts of him
where I could no longer see they were him.

But even in high summer, he heals;

roughage from an endless supply
creeps together, swift as rats.

I've searched under his arms, his privates, lifting and peering.
I've taken his neck apart, expectantly,
and found the same rufous shreds.

Disgust overcame me. I beat the river bottom with my fists.

He strolls carelessly close to flames
and takes delicious naps on the granite slab.

When I first climbed down here to the stream
and saw him, my regrets, as from a thousand simultaneous yanks,
snapped free.
I never left.

It Has Been, Yes

We ease into abstract wicker chairs
to discuss the latest hailstorm,

replaying all the fallen trees
as a children's choir or dawn sitar.

Our toes probe the softening ground.

There must be some postcard or parcel yet to arrive—
I like to think—
not to mention the sure-flying castles.

Blame the phantom canons they get lost.

New buffalo roam the plains. My dear, you end up shooting them
and only stop when one dies with its tongue
on the back of your hand.

At this point, you head back.
Actually, you sprint.

I've been digging a trench with the shovel you gave me.
The moment you show up, a little dirt flies in your face.
You go to pieces.

Come inside, I say. There's a nice time capsule I've been saving.

The night I can't forget, neither of us showered
nor tried to look like anybody else.
The radio station must have canceled its weekly pledge drive.
We cooked a big meal and grooved around the kitchen

like the rarest amateurs on earth.

Scout

His sentences all ended with the word Austin,
a place I'd never seen,
so I packed a duffelbag,
overwatered the garden, and set out on foot,
the way many of the greats in my family had done,
among other rascally things.

The flutter of engines enchanted me.

Most awkward moment:
Out of cash,
bartering my eyelashes.

Thank you, bad-shot farmers, for all the pecans.
Thank you, hounds, for losing interest.

Some nights I would wake to a sweet melody grinding
like an ice cream summons and stumble,

half-awake, trying to answer the phone in a forest.

So what if I drooled into rock receivers?
Someone needed to arrive first
and put an ear to the ground.

Someone needed to find a loft with flexible floors.

Who better to memorize the acoustics of local venues,
know which houses were haunted,
which gutters led somewhere?

I tumbled after the weeds,
eager to turn on the A.C.
and give the first tour.

Playing House

Right now the bed is not wide enough,
but I can still see you,
six or so inches away.

It's okay
to look into your eyes.

We don't even have to touch,
as nothing says I want you
more than looking.

You find no reason to steal,

though I am the sunken ship you've been diving for
your whole life.

At first it's too dangerous
to blink,

but I guess now that I've imagined our first few mornings,
I would also like to watch you sleep—

kind of floating
among the starfish
and the nickels.

The chink between the curtains
sets your hair on fire, you know.

I could let you out of my head,
but then you might forget something important,

like your thoughts.

You could come out chasing a soccer ball
or doing downward dog or replacing a tree.

Taiga

The globe shakes and
There you lie in snow, your eyes winged with ice and
Blue guttering lips full of smoke, and
I have cracked my teeth on chattering sips and
Flung our trinkets into groaning lakes and
Followed hints of woodsmoke, blind in a squall, and
Hummed peculiar strains to muffle familiar ache and
All to find you in this place where toes and
Hands are chewed of hearths and
Yours grown black I clamp in caves and

Down the Shore

We take mental pictures of our new commute
over the wind-deaf causeway,
comparing these to postcards of ancestral coal mines.

Soon we have named every seagull on the island,

one timid evening discovering that tuna tastes best
when smoked with pine.

You find a silk scarf the color of lemons
and leave it on my vanity table.

Twice a day, a huge truck carrying who-knows-what,
probably repossessed cities, roars past our cheerful teardown.

We make a ritual of closing the windows just in time
to keep road dust from coating the grand piano.

This piano has never been cleaned, not a single feathered swipe,
since our hero Sergei knocked at the door
and asked to use the phone.

Though he never sat down to play, didn't even enter the room.

When minnows start schooling in our basement
and night lights become all too naturalistic,
we hire our own children to prop the timber-frame up on poles,
like an upside-down cheese platter.

But the measuring tape was snapped once too often
or left out in too many thundershowers.

We rename our home The Cheese Platter anyway.

You take up spearfishing till Steve loses an eye.

Debts pile up in one way or another, and we have to find a lodger.

She is blond and telescopic, always standing temptingly
by windows, silhouetted. She beckons you
to rummage some bottomless goodie bag of irrelevant spheres.
She introduces you to crowds of bright squares.
My face hurts after a while. By then you've built an observatory.

There is dust everywhere,
except on the powerful lenses
and the farthest reaches of her galaxy.

There is dust on my corneas. I leave it there.

Our children enter strange professions
and insist on cooking for me,
while your conferences on spaghettification stretch endlessly late,
well past first light.

I demand perfect marshmallows, bhindi masala, spätzle,
fermented cordials. There will be no soup, no store-bought mayo!
Sometimes I wail so hard I retch.

No one is permitted to vacuum or move
my growing collection of razor clams
from the shelves.

One of these days I may craft a pliant frame and string them up at
various heights then hang this outburst in the foyer, which must be
crossed to get anywhere in this hellhole.

The sound whenever a person, any person, passes through
will calm me, like a chorus of reclaimed daggers,
keeping my daydreams in check.

That was the plan anyway, but today a letter arrived.
A letter from a man who calls himself Simon.

Simon heard about my collection
from his trespassing cockatoo.
As you can see, my salvation could hardly have made sense.
No local health clubs or hypnotherapists pop up on the map.

I learn to tolerate this parrot squatting on the rim of my tea saucer
as Simon holds me on his lap.

He holds me on his lap and cleans my face with a cloth.

One cloth after another.

Eventually, I have nothing more to say but
Are you hungry yet?

Therapy

The waterfall looked more fed up than regal.

In the shadow of a hemlock,
two people shouted,
chest to chest

like sea lions.

~

Insults flew.

Meteors flashed close to the ground.

Barnacled explosives beached themselves.

A gang of toys brandished their "press-here"s.

~

You kick books out of bed like it's your job!

The least suggestion sends you behind glass!

Those costumes aren't convincing!

No more applause! My hands are striking!

~

Every treehouse in the universe creaked
on the verge of collapse
then collapsed.

21

~

Some catbird mouthed off.
The moon sprang up uninvited.

She thought but didn't say.
He responded without knowing it.

Their clothes left microscopic traces on leaves.

They trudged back to the car
and, hours later, continued looking.

When Honeysuckle Wine Comes in Boxes

We meet at the end of a boulder-strewn trail,
not exactly the top of a mountain.

There could be a sweeping view somewhere,
but the blank petals and paint cans trifle with it.

Child-proofed bees hum in our glances.

By chance, we remembered an assortment of brushes:
sable, badger, polyester.

I like to watch your conducting motions
from behind the striped tent,

especially when you're airbrushing the meadow and savvy.

But I wish you wouldn't poison the rosebushes at night
just to see how I will look at eighty.

Our tenderest moments generally happen at midday
and when you stoop below the brim of my hat.

With the passage of months, you develop a rash
that bubbles as I talk.

Mornings grow chilly. I drape my arm around you—
you swallow your tongue.

On a patch of grass flattened by deer,
I spend hours summoning song lyrics.

Another great cruise ship enters the harbor.

I desert you.

There are decades of flat water.
I tumble perky strawberries into a bowl to eat at a table, alone.
Light whistles everywhere.

You happen to be aboard the same vessel, on the same deck,
in the same dining hall,
but you always did like cantaloupe.

Our spotless tablecloths turn against us.

Bugs under the Stream Rocks

They live on the river bottom in the cold clear motion
near the cave unstuffed with bodies and the new development.

What's ahead? Behind are fleecy corridors
you swore were full of people.
You heard them joking,
heard them murmur.

We drove up a president's mountain,
made tea with weeds in the September rain.

When you listened, I grew fins.
When you stopped,

Kleenex ate the world.

Big deal you're loyal to your obese Australian shepherd.
Cake more mud on your boots for anonymity's sake.
No one strides with more sophisticated boyishness over roots—low
branches flicking back—than you.

So whittle me another anecdote,
you mimic of Mercury.

Blameless kaleidoscopian!

Or let's stay in all week and read missing person reports.

Last year, while I lay on the grass
taking panoramas, there was a ten-minute period
you were a statistic,

but your depressballs basement photo is everywhere now.

I don't remember your mouth.
Perhaps I haven't tried enough.
Your face is smooth.

I like the planet you were made for.
I think I was made for that rock pile too.

And while you pace your apartment,
a scrapbook of maple leaves disintegrates.
Pick one up and the world clouds over.

All you ever tell me are ghost stories of the living breathing.

In the kitchen of well-ground loneliness,
sugar ants touch each other
constantly.

The Remaining Years

Lily's lover makes a few passes through the murk.
Finally he crashes the plane.

The piano titters, good and loud.
Someone else eats his steak.

His watch ticks down,
and Lily weds a traveling knife grinder.

She asks him to shave his mustache, but he won't.

White lines lengthen overhead . . . . She conjures up
different-looking kids not feeding hens and geese.

The holes her mother jabbed to decorate her ears close,
and her neighbors do all the talking.

One day a rusty lawn chair collapses beneath her.
Peas scatter from the bowl.

When her husband dies, she rents a piano,
but her fingers on the keys fall like drips on stone.

Too long ago.
Too long to go.

Acid reflux climbs her throat in low scrapes everyone ignores.

Inside red glass, the candle gutters as
her great, great grandchild runs through the house.

His hand is pried open.

Relatives pass the watch around,
then take it to an expert, who sees straightaway
nothing remarkable.

The streets have been paved. The vendors have moved indoors.
Every block smells oddly sweet of hamburger.

Taking Stock

In memory of my grandmother, Johanna Madeline Sonye

The legend of a single yellow canary.
The fact of the small house that says nothing but has history.
The legend of glass that cracks exactly how it should.
The legend of Mother Nature tossing in her sleep.
The fact of following the other kids until you wonder why.
The fact of one word for certain things and hundreds for others.
The fact of wrecking a night's work without breaking stride.
The fact of hoping things turn out right.
The legend of recognizing when they have.
The fact Grandma sewed and crocheted many presents for me.
The legend of bark dust spinning in the bend of a river.
The legend of sweating it out.
The fact of shivering flowers.
The fact of parenting.
The legend of instructions.
The legend of two bowls of cereal and a banana every morning.
The legend of bananas in heaven.
The legend of breathing.
The fact of pollen.
The legend of meeting one's Al.
The statistical odds.
The legend of her lying in a crib dreaming away.
The fact of mostly expecting to see her today anyway.
The legend that she is feeling the same way.
The legend of belonging to a vibration and a place.
The fact of a cool breeze.
The fact of not remembering every moment and that being okay.
The legend of experience as a series of twists and kinks.
The fact of hazel eyes and hi-gloss penny loafers.
The fact of noticing beauty even when you're really tired.
The legend of a hole-in-one swing.

Fists Pound with Appetite

Fists pound with appetite. Bring the net and ladder.
Licorice won't help. Nor brief journeys from island to red island,
costing starlight. Drag the net under my drowned fancy.
Assistant, yes with the limp, pass a rope through some eyelets.
Now haul me up. You figure it out. This is paramount.
Glasses of whatever won't help. Nor meeting deadlines.
Dripping sweat, nope, sorry. I must be saved by a nonentity!
Suspend me over this preposterous quantity of water.
Turn up the moon. Now hide it partially. Speak
names I've never heard. Keep them coming.
Handles well out there, ungraspable. Search banks and bars,
firths and coral. I will hover so until the spent adhesive outlook
and the twitch blow away. If there is morning, it breaks late.
If clouds rain, the drops pace themselves. My skin shines
then goes away. Because railings won't do it.
Because just quilts can't help. Because, you, assistant
with the loose tongue like an unloved button, must go fetch
pillowcases full. Do not come back otherwise.
If you can, forget coming back at all. Go now.
Make your encounters.

That's Some Muddy Water

cleaning your clothes.
That's some cheap wine
corking up my nose.
And it's good to be back.
I have to say that though
this has never been my home.

That's a bold mouse taking a stroll.
That's a long CD I've never heard,
while figs fall on the roof and
a quail roo calls from the tree.
Nothing urgent, just swell
to have vanished mid-thrashing
from the world.

Fold

A wagon of body parts has tipped over
and spoiled your precious rock garden of ordinary life.

Take a single blank sheet of 8½" x 11" paper.

Start by lining up the corners.

If the paper is crinkled or coffee-stained, whatever.

Ignore all orbs.

By this point, you should have a delicious tear-shaped tunnel . . . .
Collapse and flatten it with the edge of your hand.

Now set this on a high shelf to yellow.

The topside should feel faintly gritty when you unfold
and halve the paper
down the crease.

If your tear wanders off on some brainless errand,
don't go burning down a forest. Sheesh.

This is just a thing you do sometimes—another thing
no one has to know about.

Keeping It Down

You turn the knob slowly, float the door closed with a wince.
But your ankles, like wicker, out-cavil the stairs.
Creaking fits of bone-sneeze, you steal down the runner,
toilet unflushed, silk robe aflutter.

We kids strain for noise-plumes of morning cartoons,
hypnotized with eyes glued to loud-looking japes.
Acme co. backfires with full orchestra guarded low.
You whisper, "lower." We cringe at the ceiling and obey.

You heat hard water in a voiceless kettle,
steep thanks kept fresh in Grandma's battered tin,
sip milky consolation, watch the backlit coils of steam,
while our patriarch upstairs scours beds of shallow dream.

Morning in My Hotel

The view is born a boy
with crows in his hair

I am watching a breeze lick the dead
and living gorse and grilling my thighs
on the radiator

From far-off
comes a sound like a conch blast
or piping on monster reed

I lever out the window catch and let the cold inside

its parasitic noise
a cow with overtones

thirsty

The crow on the pole stabs a mystery with its face

Cue the marimba arpeggio

Mouth

While traveling
a lot changes

in one's mouth

Some people have short tongues
very short tongues

Others have long bottom jaws

Each of us has a most comfortable batch of sounds

a wet library of favorites
caged birds in the garden

My mouth wants to split itself apart, lips yes but also the hinges of
my jaw as though looking for a tight corner to bark from

People like to ask
where did you grow up

They want to decide which of my sounds belong

Adapting

My ideals are horrified. My ideals never leave the soil.
Hit tunes say even less than what hurts a mosquito's ego.
I could sit and watch the sea gull watch mud all day,
but get-togethers must occur as planned and people can't abide
drinking plain water. It's hard knowing whether to speak
when the divide sums up years of respective mediocrity.
Also the exhaustion of seeing nearly every relationship turn
machine and break down. The trick is retrieving the consummate
feeling that accompanied knowing no one's opinion mattered.
All while being too much in everyone's gaze. As hours get
whittled into seconds and bodies into lines, I don't like what comes
to mind to say. Inevitably, some noise must be made.
Turning experience into a pantry of approximates,
something cooked on high for one minute.

In Our Cabin

Grandfather, while you were out checking traps,
a brown bear pushed in the door

He took a seat by the stove and ate
the last loaf of bread

My kitten was ricocheting around room with her tiny sickles out
until the bear, tired of surprises, flicked his paw

Now she is just a little fur island with no one there

Please be more careful, I said
slopping the tea

But I forgot to add the leaves

With a grunt, the bear plucked her still-warm lump off the ground
and peeled it

masterfully

I know, Grandfather, from watching you work
I had to learn
not to read each face,

like learning not to overhear

I wished that we could put all those pink bundles back
inside their mothers with a message not to let them out again
until the day of judgement,

but you scolded me for speaking bad luck

The bear said I invited him in
He left the chrysolite to prove it

Collector

The first prayer I ever made up:

Please take care
of each evicted turtle,
smeared opossum,
white deer ballooning hard
on the route to school.

For Christmas one year I took the tongue from a rotting fawn
and put it in a Red Bird box of matches.

I gave this to my uncle who collected skulls—
a meringue to go with acorns.

Years later I would hallucinate
animals where they didn't belong:

A janitor ransacked the cafeteria for a dog;
a close friend drove back to find the road pure.

These visions were nothing outrageous,
not Nazis or aliens.

Though some were unearthly.

On Venice Ave.
the spongy cones of light
never made it past a certain bend.

A thing leapt at me
over the front wheel of my bicycle,
a huge black wolf.

I survived.

Jackdaw

In the torn evening, joggers and pensioners move around.
I watch your yellow eyes—

two distant, tiny beads. That wing is all wrong.
Like a sash it crooks across your breast.

A girl with her hair yanked back decides not to see
and you throw your body, ruined though it is, to one side.

Will those friends of yours not flap down and if not croak the rites
then nod as you nod? Who made them

so callously wise as not to roost this night with you
on the wet sod, tempting foxes?

I imagine first light, a rustling of leaves
being slung in a pile, your last, wondering glance.

Exchange

Children once played under clouds of raucous black.

Now strollers have puncture-proof shields.

For months, I recorded
the croaks, clicks, and pebble-trills of crows,
ascribed them phonemes, speculated on their meanings.

My hair lost its luster to bark dust
as I documented one thousand rasped ideas, then another hundred,
then another thousand....

Their rants felt like home,
their sparkling, feast-stupid looks
suspended our cruel earth.

It rained buttons, pen caps, and broken mirrors.
They'd seen people parading junk.

Eventually, the institute cancelled my project,
and busybodies crowded the understory.

I cawed at them to fuck off. They laughed.

Hatchlings toppled with questions,
everything from traffic lights to rotating doors.

I summarized *Casa Blanca,*
and they shat on the ending.

These were the early days,
before crows flocked near bank machines
and the Department of Fish and Wildlife
resorted to poisoned roadkill.

This is my deli.
Business has been so-so.

See on the roof? That's Felix.

He's fluent in English, but hasn't said a word since his mate
fell from the air.

Her wings shook leaves from the trees
and made nighttime visible.

Still

The tree that kills you
cannot leap out of the way
of your bright lights

or loose its rings before impact,

so it continues to breathe
in its secret noseless fashion

and to roam underground for minerals,

the bruise of that huge instant pressure
like a blotch of stopped time.

Perhaps it feels your disturbance most
on days the wind tests the branches
and whips the faded ribbons

or possibly during the night,
shifting quietly
within itself.

Storm

First we saw the rough shell's edge of the cloud bank
descend and glide in close,
and as we kissed hello by afterthought
the thunder knocked gently.

Now the egrets stick together,
like the rings of the shower curtain flailing,
on the stolen footholds of spartina.

A herring gull dips its head through a gust,
as the creek turns white-gummed
and our little house wobbles.
Someone's bike falls over.

Purple martens splice into the cedars.
A tern dives toward a log only to lose a hundred yards.

When the wind dies, a blackbird tuts in relief
or defiance or almost as if to do a headcount.

Shadow

I am taller,
he compacter.
More defer-faced am I,
he routine thrusts of snout.
Lips for me are grey
or calendar velvet. For him, black blending into pink,
punctuated white. I have skin that shows
the forfeits of living.
He wears countless tassels
of slipped-by-unnoticed gold.
When sleep sinks onto us, I stretch flatter, he balls up.
My palms are false maps.
His span ready-made archipelagoes.
Prim of limb, often quoting smells,
his hackles scuff the air. A howling prime example!
My own neck will ladle itself to death.
Absent with me, minute by hour,
requiring what he requires—
the needy, brown-eyed question
teaching me how to exist.

Visit

It was my first time in a Toys "R" Us.

As I tried to hug an ostrich
in the fourth aisle on the right,

tubes and wires stabilized
my student.

All semester she had crept to and from the last row,
smiled, and said *bye*, her grammar mostly correct,
her heels three inches high.

The ostriches were smug
and easily strangled.

I pondered the rabbits,
but she probably hadn't read *Watership Down*.

Stupid, she would describe the damage she had caused herself
those long evenings with the radio playing, alone in her room.

None of the several canine breeds gave kisses
or turned in circles before quieting down.

The owls cared too little; the teddies' fur was green;
the crocodiles had teeth; the pandas were going extinct.

At some point during my visit,
a white parking meter would roll up to her cot.
Initially, we wouldn't understand this was the doctor,
fully certified and battery-powered,
with lens, mic, screen, and tiny screws.

This one plush grizzly might have crossed icy streams,

lurked just off the trail—who knew what it had seen,
or would dream

beside her, lying low
till spring.

A Quiet Evening of Leftovers

None of the emotions of the actors are relevant
or understandable anymore,

except the one who arrives home from the hospital, friendless,

his silhouette black against the constant light of the hallway.

Will he turn on the lights when he shuts the door?
Or just approach his bed, face away from it, bend his knees,
and droop from the edge?

Will the idea of actually lying between the sheets,
like a person with tomorrows,
call for a splash of—really? Rosé?

It goes to show how little we know of
those we miss throughout the day.

More questions glare in.

Which acquaintances like to be disappointed? Which know better
than to kill the volume? Where is the ice thick?

He imagines a time before thought decorated itself
with mirrors, fragrant soap, and apologies,

a time of jumping fences
and storms of slapstick,

before the notion of long-term effects became a thing.

While unconscious, his soul was atom-blasted and refitted
with an aphid's or a scrap of cardboard from the future.

He reads about a hostage situation. There was a girl
the victim intended to call, a specific reason
to jump from the car.

His phantom limbs cartwheel.

Somebody's Neighbor

In love he was his worst.

He raised his hand to dogs
and skinned his palms

going down the slide.

It's been a while since the cumuli
of ever after.

Dusting himself off takes a lot of extra pats.
You name it—he's fractured it,

squinting through the horror.

Between greeting cards,
he's run out of color.

No one notices the empty walk-in closet
he now uses to shake hands.

Occasionally, while the cat scratches its pan, he'll remember
how other kids reinvented sand, screamed
fountains on a windy day.

Where did his super powers go?

The slide keeps shrinking and promising less,
losing rungs, squeaking under his heels.

There are still dogs clipped to the fence
that whine and loll their tongues.

He lets them lick the blood, past and future, from his hands.

Doppelgänger

The botanist had reams of leaves
and hives like newsprint
and fame.

One day an identical man walked up to him.

The identical man was polite but drooled
from the same corner of his mouth.

Excusing himself,
the botanist found a seat in the back of the auditorium,
while his twin squelched passionately into a microphone
about a moss-dwelling mauve and white flower.

The botanist's ears started to shrivel.
He wanted to die, or at least disappear
into a jungle.

No one else seemed bothered.
Many looked bored, others thrilled

by the splashing of a thing,
then things, that flopped onto the podium:

little peanut bunker in a school.

The speaker explained how the flowers could be smoked
to revive a dead fondness and other leechcraft uses.

The fish from his mouth explored the floor uphill,

where a number of spring-breakers and antiquarians
were busy booking flights and building towers of postcards.

The fish jumped into their laps and nibbled them
down to the bones, which were white.

The botanist bit his finger and wished it could fire.

The fish reeked.
The cleaned travelers percussed themselves.

He ran out and wrote fifteen utterly sincere emails
to the people who understood him best.

There was a knock at the door.

Here

Someone close to me has been dead a while.

We never met
but,

we were supposed to.

When I first heard of him,
his ulcers were common knowledge.

No one seemed concerned.

His lap looked warm and uncomplicated,
like lo mein,

his rough brown clothing
ragged and friendly

enough to nuzzle without leaving a stain.

We never quite met,
though I heard

we were inseparable.

He recognized my ever fantasy and sigh,
whether I was asleep or pretending, intending to rest my head
on the shoulder of a boy.

I got so used to looking at the world as a meal

whipped up under the sky,
here and there underdone,

the edges a little burned,
often stale

—but good!

The cook has died.

Plates continue to arrive.
No one called about the funeral.

Can you imagine?

But there isn't enough gravel to fill all that . . . .
It would rain down on our faces.

We would bury ourselves!

No one offered a shoulder. No one noticed anything wrong
when this friend I had never met officially,
never exchanged a private smile with

passed on.

I want to press my face into his scalp and smell the decay.

Who will guide me, set the stage with a meadow in pots,

hire a kind man with soft, freckled hands
to say a word or two,

let my snot cling to his afternoon clothes,
his drool land in my hair

as the certainty of acquaintance goes by the wayside,

lifts like fog and nothing changes

except that no one
was recently

here?

Episode

At midnight in a dirt parking lot
dust won't settle

Too late for pianissimo therapy
and passionflowers

Something tells her lungs don't wait
go now

hurry

*

Cells speak from across the river
with megaphones

Each wants
its own bunk in the ship
in a bottle

Save them move them they are tired of each other

Thems the rules

Anubis?

*

There must be a beach
where no road leads

a place as yet unnamed

Iridescent bricks protect it

from far away

Low and high tides don't exist

Here a line in sand keeps
forever

Sinkhole

The hour arrives of illicit shadow puppets,

summer juries barking
in tiki torch light.

Scenery: gritty floors,

hydrants of sweat.

Hear death trot his pristine gutters,
the tinkling of muds,

wizard of messy removals.

Build a mantel with these unintended bones—

teeth
for the ceiling popcorn,

marrow summoned up the stack
to drift along

metaphysics.

Quiver and sing
Oh candy!

Oh monstrous rewards!

So bright with microscopic morgues . . . .

Loved me more than breath she said.

Who?

Who was it she meant?

Some decades.
Some structures occasionally
chomped
apart.

Sometimes in the half-light,
Custom Knife-Making stares innocently from the shelf.

Conifers sway where they will die.

How special to bleed
the right amount.

Special Forces

For Anton

Another day breaks in the hectic desert.

Flowers flash.
Skeletons count change.

Only when the sun hangs directly overhead
is it quiet.

I'm learning to love the desert.

Nothing else will thirst or crack for me.

The desert stocks its shelves.
The desert fills its calendar.
The desert looks travelers in the eye and says,

I'm clean.

There was a man that tied himself to a tree and trekked around and
around in the snow until help arrived.

But where did he pretend to go?

No one is coming for me, so this is extremely important.

I want the desert to wake up and shake itself out.

Wake up, I hiss

until it's time to sleep.

Nowhere

For Beth

You know what I like? Cold cotton sheets
when my skin has turned to lichen with itching.
I love draping them around my shoulders and hips
and going back to a time before seams.
I like throwing a last-thread gaze skyward
when the dog has paced me from an untried thought
to hurry me down the block and seeing
how clear the dark is, sandy with stars, how electric
lines cut right above us like inadequate yarns
I tell the birds sincerely. I like being dismissed
for no obvious reason and not making it my business.
I didn't used to, but my nature finally showed up,
stained the rug, and broke the heirlooms.
I watch the rest sidle off or don't.
There have been times none of this was happening,
times carefully devastated, too terrified of their passing.
Now when my anticipation, lying down too
quickly, back rolls, I go with it.

A Frozen Summer

Zorabelle surfaced, marvelously solid.

She gained favor among the downcast,
humoring the out-skilled, embracing the daunted.

Bare soil became Lesson #1.

We lay on our bellies, studying handfuls
of boulders aged down to specks.

We climbed tall pines and scooched into their tassels,
following each resinous hope until
it bowed us toward our forebears.

The price to stay where we had grown made us
unrecognizable,

so we left our Land of Motion Detector Lights.

Proponents of karmic promptness
were our most psychological haranguers.

(One sage from Portugal compared them with
tubbed eels trying to out-slip each other.)

Former delights crippled me from time to time—cocooning
armchairs, frogs in waistcoats, drop cookies, mild weeding.

Whenever a strange child peered into the two-room tent
and saw me thus hamstrung, I shook my head vigorously.

Zorabelle had not come to make us influential
or effective sleepwalkers, but to observe our pangs as we would
blooms and nullities of fireworks at the far end of a lake.

She sat opposite me and dealt the cards—
velvet-backed with faces of the sky—and said, "How beautiful
you are," pointing to a steel crag of weather.
"This is you about to rain."

When I had wandered off and cried myself hilarious,
the landscape where we had camped
(a mown strip under high-tension wires) crisped into
a lightly-made battleground shimmering
with one-of-a-kind mistakes.

We danced many nights to ocarina and tambourines.

Frequently, an article that no one had improved or bothered with,
like a stump, a swampy tennis ball, or someone's sock,
turned holy for a few minutes, and we would leap and stamp
in its honor, the newcomers hanging back, scathed.

On Route 30, behind a boneless farmhouse,
Zorabelle noticed my affection for X.

We swayed that night for a sacred shingle of asbestos.
Then Zorabelle pointed her finger at me, a test:

to watch X spin and ripple no more fervently
than he had for some debris.

The musicians stayed in-pocket as I fled,
cramped with feedback from the world's motion,
skin gone, heart speeding toward explosion,
mind become a tourist who promptly drowns.

Come morning, a puddle showed my face against the sky.

Chatter

No one has lived here in decades, but now I do,
so I shift the bookshelves when it rains
to catch soup from the ceiling, catch punch.
I nail the upstairs blankets so the top one falls loose,
like a focusing hood, letting me under to revel privately
in the bareness of the ocean. As temperatures fall,
the dog and I keep bonding, folded up like tacos
in comforters and wool. He's smart enough to stay there
while I boil water and crouch in the bath before work, keeping on
and steeping my sweater, listening to the plastic on the windows
not do its job, not hold out the outside air. Some kook left
a perfectly good—only slightly rusted—50mm telescope here,
so the other night as the moon, like an unfelt cut, cropped up,
I climbed to the roof of a neighbor's, a house more abandoned just
newer, and shimmied, scrunch-faced, outside the atmosphere.
In the distance, a humid light swallowed me. Then I swallowed it.
But how to show this? In summer, when eyelashes reflect inside
your shades, only thick as tree trunks, and you become
a river observing some arid basin it once carved . . . .
This morning the wind has knuckles, and the knocking sounds
urgent. It may be time to nail more blankets up, say so long
to daylight's stencils on the floor, exaggerating paned openness,
as my friend up the street claims people in this town keep doing
to his rear. He sees more than I do and suffers for it,
aware that we do not belong by the shore,
can't afford it, simply put, not even at medium wage,
not the way most bosses micromanage. Just floating in the surf,
he gets screamed at by fishermen, their rods rigged
with invisible flags of dominion, flags that can't but whip
a light-footed sloth, an unambitious moss, in the face,
as it gets colder and colder then warmer then snows.

Mission

I've been wandering in and out of paw prints.

A blind boy hauls me from one such crater.

We build a fire that burns high enough
to latch light to his eyes.

My dog yowls from close by.

Storms of forgotten villagers turn my description of the mongrel
into uncontrollable gesture
as they spin me closer and closer to their crystals.

Soon I have my own life story mixed up.

Eventually, they congratulate themselves nonspecifically
and leave me atop a mountain of bare shelves,

the craftsmanship varied,
all of it wrecked.

The murky corners of the particle and hard woods grow into
ancient faces whose solutions have plinked out of fashion.

It takes concentration not to twist an ankle
and become the resident tchotchke.

The flicker of an orange snout within the pile
bids me burrow down.

Goddamn—there's so much chaos to root around!
So much muck and blame. Strings popping. Rancid consolations.

The shelves are pieces of shit

for not holding this shit against the wall.

The center of the earth is a buttery gold sponge
and as warm or cold as a token apology.

Everything can be found here.
Here only, but everything.

Acknowledgments & Notes

Acknowledgments and thanks to the editors of the following publications, where some of these poems first appeared.

The Belleville Park Pages: "Taiga"
Field: "It Has Been, Yes," "Episode"
Love within Love: "Here"
Map Literary: "Down the Shore"
The New Yorker: "Scout"
Quarryman: "Morning in My Hotel," "The Remaining Years"
The Rutherford Red Wheelbarrow 8: "Collector,"
  "A Quiet Evening of Leftovers"
Steps Magazine: "Keeping It Down,"
  originally "Another Quiet Morning"
The Stinging Fly: "Mouth," "In Our Cabin"

Thanks also to Todd Swift of Eyewear Publishing for selecting "Chatter" for a Fortnight Prize.

I am grateful to my parents Kevin and Rosemarie, my partner Jeffrey Perkins, and to the many incredibly kind people who have offered support along the way, including Maeve Bancroft, Charles Clements, Bill Conall, Emari DiGiorgio, Waleed Mahmoud Ebeid, Jim Klein, Mona Knight, Beth Mann, Mary Morrissy, Rick Mullin, Kathleen O'Brien, the late Michael O'Brien, Minga O'Brien, Patrick O'Flaherty, Kate Oland, Barry O'Sullivan, Leanne O'Sullivan, Niamh Prior, the late Matthew Sweeney, Anton Yakovlev, and the wonderful Red Wheelbarrow Poets and World Above Poets.

"Special Forces" is for Anton Yakovlev.

"Nowhere" is for Beth Mann.

The title poem is a fictional continuation of the life of a minor character in Howard Hawks' 1939 film *Only Angels Have Wings*.

About the Author

Bridget Sprouls was born in New Jersey and educated at McGill University, Le Conservatoire de Musique de Québec, and University College Cork. Her poems have appeared in *The Belleville Park Pages*, *Field*, *Map Literary*, *The New Yorker*, *Steps Magazine*, *The Stinging Fly*, and elsewhere. A recipient of Eyewear Publishing's Fortnight Prize, she spends her time between Cape Breton and New Zealand. This is her first collection of poems.

www.ingramcontent.com/pod-product-compliance
Lightning Source LLC
LaVergne TN
LVHW041309080426
835510LV00009B/923